MW00783312

ANDERSON BOOKWORKS

PRESENTS

CURTAINS

A Spiritual Penning

By

John Anderson

Publishing.........Covenant Books
Publication Coordination.........Renee Barnhill
Cover Design.........John Anderson and Maxi Vittor
Illustration.........Elizabeth Gallego and Anastasiya Iskakova
Editing and Page Design.........Publication Staff at Covenant Books

ISBN 978-1-63885-591-0 (Paperback)
ISBN 978-1-68526-713-1 (Hardcover)
ISBN 978-1-63885-592-7 (Digital)

Covenant Books
11661 Hwy 707
Murrells Inlet, SC 29576
www.covenantbooks.com

To Ruth Hill—
an inspiration and a warrior before I ever was

PROGRAM

Act I: Curtains

Scene I: Dark Beginnings

Scene II: Fighting Back

Scene III: Messages of Hope

Scene IV: Love and How to Find It

Scene V: Love and the Return of Politics

Scene VI: The Believers Get Their Fair Share

Scene VII: Death of a Poet

SCENE I

•

DARK BEGINNINGS

i.

I feel the darkness of the world that lives.
Scared and ominously cautious.
The stress fills the air, suffocating all.
No one dare go outside.
The shadows of demons follow, bride and not alike.
But they cannot touch the saved.
No, not all are saved! Not all are saved!
Chaos ensues.

Come in, all children. Come in.

Children: always afraid of the dark, but God's are the light.
The world claws and looks for a home: the safe space.
But we have found our home, in our place.

I feel for the people.
God and Satan's alike.
We all seem lost; we are not so different.
We are all humanly supernatural.

Some walk with angels, and some with devils,
But now the devils turn on their friends.
Angels walk among their allies; do not fear, do not fear!
For the believer: be brave and rejoice.
The coming of the Lord is near.

ii.

Lord of the flies?
Lord of the lies.

There is only one Lord, and with Him, we rise.

iii.

Here is the case of the struggling man:
It's quite complex, so keep up if you can.
He sits in his pew, entrapped in his art.
Always distracted, when preaching will start.
True he means well. Write? He must.
But is it right, proper, timely, or just?

He is cursed, how sad; no one understands.
Well, no one on earth, look to God's hands.
They sit and they sit, talking to one another.
They are close friends; brother and brother.
They talk of his purpose to understand this man.
Yet though the man sits, he tries to stand.

Oh, how God is patient, silently shaking his head.
"I know," the man says. "Without you, I'd be dead."
Thus, the man struggles, on and on,
But do not fret, dear reader.
For soon.
He'll be gone.

iv.

God has closed the world.
Can't you see?
He's closed the world,
For you and me.

V.

In this life, I have discovered: We get what we deserve.
If you are to be a fool, then foolishly you are rewarded.
Heroes take a hero's journey as well as the villains.
For without a villain, there is no hero.

Only a soul destined for greatness it cannot achieve.

Yet a villain can suffer all the same.
In a world so obsessed with heroes and villains, I ask:
"Which am I?"
I know I claim to be a son of God, yet I act so undeserving.

What is it to be a hero or a villain?
It is to get what you deserve in the end.

vi.

Six feet apart, six feet apart.
How we strive to be together.
Six feet apart, six feet apart.
Like birds of the same feather.

Six feet apart, six feet apart.
God's eagles up in their nests.
Six feet apart, six feet apart.
Tarry, be safe, enjoy, now rest.

Six feet apart, six feet apart.
Anxiety follows the chosen few.
Six feet apart, six feet apart.
Fear not; angels watch over you.

Six feet apart, six feet apart.
God speaks: "Children, have no fear.
Though you may be six feet apart,
I, your God, draw ever more near."

vii.

The seventh seal is nearly open.
Do you have the Lord's token?

viii.

As the world turns, so does the Son.
Who am I to disagree?
Circumstances unnatural we can't outrun.
Though confusing, God is with thee.

As the world turns, the Sun will go down.
It is the way of our creation.
Night will fall, darkness surrounds.
Glory train leaves the station.

Jesus Himself had to face death.
It will come, we can't deny.
Don't forget the God who gives breath,
He forgets not you and I.

Even in death, we find God's plan.
Unknown, but holy-divine:
"Understand, my children, look at my hand,
what you're losing wins souls in time.

Though my Son leaves this earth, know this: it was not in vain.
I hold His life, knowing what it's worth; knowing the sorrow
    and pain.
Come close, my children, come close. Want to see Him again?
Of your life, I require the utmost; how I long to be your friend.

There is time to mourn and time to fear; time for all in all.
Hear me, children, for I draw near, and to the rest of you I call.
Brother, sister, mother, father: I know each one by name.
To many I am the comforter, to you I'll be the same."

I know right now it's dark.
The devil comes with lies.
The Lion's roar beats the devil's bark, for Jesus Christ did rise.

The world turns, it must by nature, but only to make way.
Foresee the night: a cold glacier the Son-rise melts away.

The Son had fallen, no time to clock, look to Christ you'll see.
Deathly conqueror, solid rock, maker of the free.

ix.

The thoughts of the devil's wile against me, but I will not crum-
    ble, my God is almighty.
He makes the devil tremble.

Though my battle rages on each day, I fear no loss,
In the midst of evil, I say, "Jesus's blood is on the cross."

Come all evil, come all hell, you are known to come anyway;
I have word from God to tell: "He is alive this very day."

The battles long, but I don't mind, pick the brain with delight.
Victory's simple, get thee behind, you've lost in every right.

How is it:
To be destined to fail.
Is that why you are driven?
Why you gnash and wail?

It is not easy to win this war.
Each battle a soul to claim.
My God knows He's fighting for me,
And I, for Him, the same.

You can come with all you've got,
The damage you will do.
But know this battle is not for naught,
The Lord, risen, is true.

X.

The love of God comes calling still.
Will I answer?
Knowing many ways and many forms,
I see what my future holds.
God's grace stands in perfect will,
Yet I falter?

"You wish to defy the norms."
No.
That's a lie often told.
My fate blows with a warm chill.
For I,
A creature?

A caged monkey who ill performs.
How can I be so bold?
My fears amass, my decisions I kill.
Am I worthy of thy daughter?
I have faced hell's mighty storms.
I am worn, my soul to mold.

With every storm a land is filled.
Do I forget my master?
My devils all will mourn.
When I,
To them,
Turn cold.

With what gift does my heart fill?
The jewel in my crown won't falter.
Worries of mine, all adjourn.
To God, we are sold.

xi.

"To be certain of God."
A bold statement still.
But what is certainty,
If not God's will?

Faith and love carry us.
God calls for this.
Have no fear and sound mind.
Gifts be not missed.

I have no fear, only doubts.
The devil has his due.
Thomas, my middle, you define my character.
But God lives ever true.

Peace is certain, approaching fast.
Does this scare or encourage?
End of days, you are the interpreter.
Give us reckoning-courage.

But as I live, I see the gift.
The act of God in life.
There she stands ever near.
Relieve my burden and strife.

xii.

What am I to You, my Lord?
Am I loving still?
Do You hear my pleading prayers,
Or are they lost in my lacking?

I long for You as devils long for me,
Battle of souls rages on.
The war is Yours, and Yours is mine.
Fight the good fight, they say.

I crumble in my loneliest pain.
How I fail You still.
Rest within my heart for soul.
I need You within.

Will I feel love from a mortal friend or love of a wife whom
        longs?
Maybe not, but in You, there is love.
And my heart is Yours.

I seek You first though distractions dismay.
I know I am foolish.
Your mercy rains supreme,
Upon my tainted soil.

xiii.

They march closer to world peace,
but in this life,
the greatest peace to be granted
is death.

xiv.

In the mirror: lies; reflection.
Am I all I say I am?
One must ask, and the one is me.
No one else can.

My tongue is silver as the sharpened sword, burning with fire
    as heated metal.
A double-edged sword, I don't possess.
One sword, one mind;
Ungrateful I've become.

Discern the spirits? Blasphemy.
I am only young and old.
I understand so little.
I know the spirit of God.

Does God's spirit know me?

I stray further from humanity.
My crutch: I am human.
It is easy to accuse, easy to judge,
Easier to judge ourselves.
God is the Judge, knowing our merits. He is almighty.
I am nothing of any sort; I am a humbled leper.

Arrogant once, likely again.
Save me from my ways.
I: a destroyer, no maker.
I: broken; a pot fallen from grace.

You: my maker who knows my ways.
Repair me stronger than before.
I am your work.

Replace my silver tongue with gold, hold me closer still.
Show me ways of love, not ways of hate and judgment.
Fill my heart with love.
Your spirit, only.

Evil spirits run aplenty; this I know is true.
But you are God, walking with me.
Love, always new.

Bring us together, cliques broken, body, together, as one.
Every piece to bring their bread and battle, side by side.

Act, every moment now, unto the evening time.

XV.

O h the joy that fills my soul, being in his presence.
Friends, I know it's been a while since we shared a sentence.

Here we are in this place, not as we were then.
Do you share this understanding?
Will you smile again?

This seems beyond comprehension,
In a land of laws and sickness,
God is King, together we stand, all here to witness.

God brings His miracles in the glint of your eyes.
My, how it looks of heaven,
Though we sit, far and wide, I say this without question.

The bread is still unleavened.
I see God in spirit and you,
I have missed you dearly, trust that this is true.

My Lord, my friends, all heavenly siblings: stay strong, do not
    grow weary.
When you smile, God smiles too.
Though masked, you cannot hide, your soul we see shines
    through.

I know my family: the chosen few.
The one they call the Bride.
We live in times of Revelations: masked, spiritually hide.

Physical types the spiritual with no hesitation,
Let your faith not be derailed.
Though separated, we are together.

My friends, my family, it's good to see you.
This poem I write anew.
I pray this finds you happy,
For I am happy too.

xvi.

Can you measure the love of God?
Can you find His equation?
We know God is a God of maths,
But barely perceive.

I am no mathematician; I am, in fact, a writer.
A man living lives, a believer of faith.
I write what I cannot read.

Can you measure the love of God?
Why would one want to?
Measurements of man are limitations
Imposed on a limitless God.

Infinite Ruler, King of Time, why must we measure?
Perhaps we need control; It is in our nature.
The nature of man is flawed, hence the purchase made for sins.
Thank the great; The Divine; The Christ for that price once
    paid.

To measure the measureless is a generous understanding.
God knowing, and knowing all, gives us the measurement.
To some, it is called simple, to others, revelation.

If you must measure love, as our minds desire to do,
Measure in the divinity of generosity.
Look at the lives of others; Look at you.

Now let this be exemplified:
Do you love mountains?
For the mountains are truly beautiful, and their beauty is
     known by the all-knowing God.

The God who knows your love of such mountains,
And thus,
Made them.

Do you love the stars?
Stars placed precisely,
In chaos for you to view.

We cannot comprehend the variables taken, the Creator's
     calculation.
Our minds are limited, let God educate you,
Though we are bad students.

To look through the eyes of God is no easy feat.
We are distracted class clowns and rebellious.
Or at war with our internal system.

But what if we were to listen to the master? To look at the lives
     we live?
The steps taken to get us here.
Imagine our surprise?

Examine your life, look for the Lord; present in the visible
     invincibility.
We cannot measure God's love,
For it is unmeasurable, unending, and undying.

Overwhelming and predestinated, know how much God loves
     you,
Suppose you don't know, even still, look at your life; others too.
The acts of God are actions of love, all you must do is see,
Gaze upon the cosmos, ye made definitively.

xvii.

Do you wish to see God smile?
Send a smile to your friend.
If you feel it's been a while, a joke is good to spend.

We know we can't see God smile; it would burn us to a crisp.
But the smile of God is within a mile, on brother's and sister's
    lips.

If you wish to see God smile, know He's smiling too,
When He sees you reconcile
With a sibling who loves you true.

xviii.

Lord, walk with me, for I cannot walk alone.

xix.

We walk in the midst of darkness, no sign of life for miles.
Demons run rampant through the streets, but we are not alone.

To be at peace in the midst of evil is peace that's true and sure.
Yet you cannot gain peace from the darkness; only God can offer.

Conquer fear and angered sadness, conquer the devils that roam.
The evils in the dark cannot win; your heart is His alone.

In the midst of darkness, we clamor for the light; we clamor for what we are.
We desire to be ourselves: God's vessels shining bright.

How ironic we do not know that we are what we seek. God places us in darkness, revealing the light to see.
A light of Him, inside of us, when times grow ever bleak. The world is dark and grown apart, yet we? The people's plea.

They wish to have the light God gave us when we are most alone; the light we choose not to see, the light more worldly known.

Believers in darkness, be not afraid; we're in the dark as light.
To all the devils we put to bed: goodbye, good riddance, goodnight.

XX.

Ah, the heart of a child, how strange they know what's mine.
For if we had the light of a child, perhaps we'd let it shine.

SCENE II

:

FIGHTING BACK

xxi.

Mighty man of God,
    Can we match your valor?
A warrior's heart, fighting still;
Strength within the battle.

Mighty man of God,
Never left in vain.
We seek to follow the vision,
You saw in God's time.

We stand upon the foundation of the lion's roar.
Every brick like every soul, placed perfectly still.

Though God is the King, we forget not His warriors.
Fighting for all, including me, God has reached me through
    you.
Though I never heard your voice, in a way I can remember.
You shaped the man that cared for me; thus, you are a father.

A father to many as the Father is still: firmly placed within thee.
Of the sons you've put in place: God is found within.
As imagination permits, I do imagine a bolt of lightning at
    birth, striking fear into a dozen devils, knowing their end
    is near.

The man-o'-war sails oceans of man, to destroy all evil.
He saves those lost at sea, pulling them aboard.
Captain of the crew, place all to station, God calls to order.
The man of war does surely listen, to every wooden border.

Speak of doctrine as you must though it is hard hearing.
With every word, a crack of lightning, igniting brush fires daily.
Burn away all evil deeds, shock us to the core.
Within our soul: holy seeds.
Let us do bad no more.

Though your name bears many doubts, I doubt it was toward
    God.
You doubted all that wasn't true, which lead God to nod.

Oh, mighty man of God, thanks are in order.
Though we know the Lord is owed, there is none without the
    other.
To this day, the Lord booms, sounding through your voice,
Teach us through your son, shake the devil's earth.
When you are gone, we will remember as we do now, I say.
Mighty man, Oh, man-o'-war:
We are your legacy.

xxii.

How ironic: Humanity has lost its humanity.
You angry few cannot see,
That hate has overcome you.

It is easy for me, a son of God, to speak of agape love.
I am used to it in my upbringing.
But what of the angry beings?

Minorities minor, majorities major, equally problematic.
God is the great equalizer,
Much like an ever-nearing death.

Only God overcomes our manmade sins.
Our acts of violence mean little.
And the little is bad.

Seek God, my friends, no act of rebellion can save you.
Surrender unto the Lord; man is not enough.
The fires of rage burn bright and are hotter still.
Hell's flames peak through the dimensions.
Can't you see the evil?

Brothers, sisters, come in peace, not in pieces.
The Lord is the comforter and the joy.
He is salvation.

xxiii.

How troublesome:
A message of love being dubbed a speech of hate.
What a brilliant lie.

Be wise in how you present the Gospel, for the world is volatile.

xxiv.

O' the joy to hear God's laughter;
A mighty chuckle from the highest mountain.
A laugh for us, His silly children,
Where else would we get our humor?

But have you heard our God bellow?
He laughs at the arrogant enemy.
O' the joy to hear God's laughter,
I smile amidst the victory.

XXV.

O Lord, come quickly.
We are ready to come home.

xxvi.

God knows who we are to love,
After all,
He loves us most.
But still love is a mystery played out perfectly and romantically.

How obscure: We determine love by chance.
Though God has control, we still gamble.
Why are we to worry?
God loves us so.
He will not leave us nor forsake us.
In prayer, we seek the answer; in prayer, we seek peace.

Be kind to yourself; do not worry.
If we are to know who will love us, we must first love ourselves.
Even God loves Himself, for we are a part of Him.

How do we love ourselves?
We must first love God.
After all, those we love bring out the best in us, and He is the
      first and last.
Once we learn to love ourselves, we are ready to love others.
Who will it be?
Only God knows.
But she will be a treasure.

xxvii.

The answer to the problem is always God, and yet we choose
another.

xxviii.

How nice it is to shred our sins like little pieces of cheese.
Melt it into a nacho dip and feed the devil disease.

xxix.

The art of poetry I will never understand.
So much reading and interpretation.
So many meanings and double meanings.
Like a maze, it is amazing.

Take what you want; that's what is written, but I never take a
    thing.
I write the words, these silly words, for someone other than
    me.

This gift I have, I've named Ironic because it's not for me.
These words I write, these metaphors, they're for you, you see?

The Bible is written as a poem,
Give it a read in pentameter.
Similarly written, by the poets of then: gifts, all for you.
I am no prophet, poet, or patriarch; I am a simple storyteller.
I find my name is only written if your day, today, is brighter.

The art of poetry, I will never understand,
I can barely make a rhyme.
But in arm's length, I lend a hand.
Until the ends of time.

XXX.

It is in man's nature to know, but the question is:
Do you?

Tree of knowledge brings the downfall, the seed of serpent
    planted.
The apple and knowledge share commonality:
Both having seeds to reproduce.

Cursed world;
Bringer of death;
The lusts of man incline.
Deadly sin earns its tithe since the beg-ending of Eden.

Regardless, there's no time,
Frugal believer, know your place.
Hold on to the oil.
Jesus arrives.

xxxi.

What is the end-time goal?
Is it not to make it home?

If it is to make it home, why do we judge?
The devil is only so much to blame.

We are held accountable for our actions, yet we choose to point
the finger.
We refuse the four pointing back; we must be better.

xxxii.

River man, river man, shaper of the rocks.
See what's within these rocks of little talks.

A raggedy pebble, mixed with gunk and rubble,
builds great beauty, in size and trouble.

Beauty inside; mineral: fluoride.
Though that would not be seen looking in from outside.

It is dirty, rough, and a heavy burden to clean.
But the river man cleanses, no matter how mean.

Cutting off the gunk and polishing the stone,
working the beauty that worked not alone.

The river man watches, tends to each stone with care,
understanding its makeup and what makes it fair.

"In you, I see gold, fluoride, and silver.
All good attributes of value, deliver."

It's hard to know what treasures are inside.
O' what beauty we ourselves do hide.

The river man knows, for he is quite witty.
He knows how we sparkle and shine so pretty.

Washed in the water and forged in blood,
carried out of darkness, rubble, and mud.

We are the rocks the river man takes:
clay, dirt, precious metals, and shapes.

Beauty within is so hard to find,
if one tries it solo with no tools to grind.

No water to clean, no diamond to graze,
no tools to chip off our filth in all ways.

River man, river man, how we need you still.
Show us, make us, the beauty you instill.

xxxiii.

How we long for love, yet God's love is longing still?
We do not wish to be alone; no one can deny.
Not even Elohim desired loneliness at the beginning of creation.

The creator of man and angels alike sat within the heavens.
A deeper connection was desired; calling, needing, still.
Angels of worship worshiped and did nothing else.
Yay, the human soul is capable of so much more.

The great creator created a profound system of love,
And the system long has fought tirelessly against Him.
The plan unchanged, completely on course, but pain: still
    persisting.
The Lord longs for our love, and we continually deny.

Longsuffering means to wait awhile, and awhile He has waited.
With this in mind, it is remarkable we do not understand our
    loneliness.
We long for the love of a spouse, yet God longs for His bride
    longer.
His patience is near unending, despite our constant troubles.

To be alone is to face overwhelming pain.
If our short loneliness is ever torturous, imagine it from the
    beginning.

We are the makers of our loneliness; we choose the path of
  little company;
We seek the kingdom of heaven, unlike the hundred millions.

How silly this simplicity evades our mentality:
If we seek the kingdom of heaven, we will have the kingdom's
  company.
In the kingdom's company, we find the King's company as well.
More so, the kingdom's population holds the spouse.

O' how we long for love though God's love is longing still.

xxxiv.

To be happy is not to be absent of pain, but to feel pain and still share a smile.

XXXV.

I cannot proclaim my own innocence.
From birth, I am the guiltiest plea.
But when the Lord is my proclamation,
He erases all guilt.

The charge is absent from my time,
And even further beyond.
We are coated in his blood,
We are drenched and redeemed.

xxxvi.

Fear is a terrible tool in the eye of the beholder.
What catches our eye is always captivating, for the actor of
    evil.

Fear is useful, masterfully crafted, to create a work of
    destruction.
Much like the subjectivity of art, we choose to see it our way.

Objectively, we are forced to see; our choice is illusive.
Yet choice stands as our own free will.

So are we to choose the masterpiece of fear, or the masterpiece
    of God?
Which is more terrible?

The mind is a powerful thing, imaginations run wild.
The thoughts strike fear through the thickest of hearts, to see
    a picture is to see what *you* see.

In fear: lies, defeat.
Yet fear is the affirmation of God's presence.

It is to His liking that He makes you greater, in the presence of
    the darkest adversary.
He desires that you overcome and rise victorious.

Challenge awakens growth, growth awakens spirituality and
spirituality strengthens the weakness that desires to haunt
you.
The devil may have tools but they are tools God has given him;
thus, they are borrowed and mastered by the Master.

They are under God's control, and I hope this brings you peace.

To be in the midst of fear is an undoubtedly terrible thing, but
to remember God is The Terrible Majesty is a gift fit for
a king.

Do not forget your maker, do not forget your purpose.
You are a child of God, shaped to be greater.

Beauty is in the eye of the beholder
Is fear truly ugly?
Though fear is present you must not forget,
It is there to strengthen thee.

xxxvii.

My faith is tested daily, and I am thankful,
I know my God is with me and carries me through the trial.

He is the challenger and defender.

He grants the adversary passage to my soul; he believes in me.
Let us make Him proud, in this final act of love.

Time is running out; eternity waits for the chosen.

xxxviii.

I am forgiven.
I am a reckless fool.
I am an arrogant man of little discipline,
And I know I must be better.

Your actions have merit.
You check me in my place.
How shameful it is that I need such action, from a long-time-
     known friend.

My friend: take me to your side.
Let me last a little longer.
Shape me as the clay that flows,
Bring me back to thee.

Let us not grow apart, my oldest and closest friend.
Life without you is nothing,
Let us come together.

In friendship and in parenthood, though there is little time,
I'd want to spend it with you.
Though I ran so far away, I am now coming home.
Slowly but surely, I return form disobedience.

You are the star; you are the light; you are all I desire.
My focus is as it should have been:
Entirely on you.

xxxix.

The corruption of democracy runs deep,
with the priests of Rome.

xl.

"What do you want in this life?"

"What do I want?"

"Yes, what do you want?"

"I suppose the new birth."

"So if that is what you want, why do you—"

"Not have it?"

"Yes, not have it."

"I haven't the slightest clue."

"I think you do. If you truly want it, then you'd have it."

"It's not so simple."

"Why not?"

"I am not worthy."

"You do not judge who is and is not worthy. I am the great decision maker. Do not play the victim when I say you're not."

"So what would you have me do?"

"Have you do?"

"Yes, have me do."

"As you are, you must begin and simply ask for it."

SCENE III

•
•
•

MESSAGES OF HOPE

xli.

Friends, if you are in the valley, know the valley matches the
    mountain,
For the mountain overlooks the valley and knows it all too well.

It takes traversal through the desert to get to the cool of the
    rock.
The desert is barren, the air is hot, cool is the mountain's top.

Friends, if you are in the valley, then now you must rejoice.
Come up higher on the mountain; it longs to hear your voice.

xlii.

It is okay to bring jo, though the world disapproves.
Some members of the church are joyless; let them not squan-
   der you.

Your joy is yours, God-given with revelation,
And countenance, made to strengthen your holy matrimony.

The joy of the Lord is your strength; be strong and of good
   courage.
Be the example the world desperately needs even if they try to
   destroy you.

As for the church folk who are as starchy as the breaded corn:
Do not bring that here.
Our joy is God-given, a precious gift, one we're willing to share.

Those of you with exceeding great joy, let us laugh together.
A smile shines with a heavenly glow when shared together with
   a feather.

xliii.

Sadness is a terrible thing; I know it all too well.
Who is exempt from such a burden?
Certainly, not I.

But to know sadness is to know God as knowing God is to
    know joy.
Sadness is but a moment,
In God's eternity.

Know this: If you are sad, you are not wrong.
You must merely remember God.
Both the moments of joy and sadness rest within His hands.

To those who see their saddened sibling, do not force your
    optimism.
Pray for your friend in their time of suffering.
Be a comforter.

When we're happy, we're happy.
When we're sad, we're sad.
If you want happiness still,
Remember God is working.

xliv.

To the mortal man, we are but a speck of dust in the sands of
    time,
Blowing in the vast breeze.
Nobody, in particular, only revealers of the jewels in our midst,
    as they brush us aside.

But to God, He remembers every grain of sand; to Him, we are
    so much more.
Valued at a price unmatched by any mortal,
To Him, we are nobody, shaped to be somebody.

Though dust will go to dust as ashes go to ashes, we are like the
    desert in which He loves to dwell:
Endless in all His precious time as an ocean that waves in the
    wind.

xlv.

We walk longingly to the good land, the land of milk and honey.
Fill us with your Holy Spirit, let us walk ever longer.

xlvi.

If I were to meet Jesus, I don't know what I'd do.
Perhaps I'd fall down crying or tell a joke or two.
But one thing I know for sure that's truly, truly true:
If I were to meet Jesus, He'd look like me and you.

Some folks might run away, in fear of all their sin.
Some might pass on out, from all the sin they're in.
Some might walk away and say, "I never knew You then."
But if I were to meet Jesus, I'd hug Him like I've been.

Now I might just meet Jesus, but what if He met me?
Would He recognize me or not know who He'd see?
I imagine He would stand awhile and smile enough for three.
He'd say, "I'd know that face anywhere. We made the devil flee."

If I were to meet Jesus, I don't know what I'd do.
Perhaps I'd fall down crying or tell a joke or two.
But one thing I know for sure that's truly, truly true:
If I were to meet Jesus, He'd look like me and you.

xlvii.

Some might think me a fool, but truly I'm misunderstood.

Though I put on a smile, it is only to protect us both.

I may be full of jokes, but my jokes are all you can handle.
If I were to be honest, our friendship would dismantle.

But since you've cast an eye this far, you know my inner
thoughts.

You know what God knows, in absolute sincerity.

This is who I am: a "humble" struggling poet.

A human all the same as you, uniquely walking with God.

xlviii.

The devil forces your surrender so he doesn't do it first.
He is the greatest swindler, but swindling cannot beat the truth.

The truth is to keep fighting, the good fight that is.
Fight like you were dying, for truth be known you are.

You are not fighting a losing battle; it is written you have won.
The devil's bones begin to rattle when he sees his fate.

The devil forces your surrender, to ensure your defeat.
Fight beside the Great Defender, and you will win the battle.

xlix.

We are marching, marching, marching to the home on high.
We're tiring and sighing, but our Lord God draws ever nigh.

1.

Evils: come cower in the dark.
Though darkness spreads within my head, I grow ever stark.
The dark you mark is stark no more; simply pulled apart.
I sit and wait while you debate, face full with a smirk.

Soldiers of the holy land: march on, march on.
Lift your heads up ever high; joyful, tag along.
Siblings, don't you worry. I know the battle's long,
We march ever closer to the land of hymnals sung.

Devils: you prosper without the light.
You make your presence known, creeping in the night.
But like roaches scatter when the light gives you a fright.
Run out of the soul that shines bright in your sight.

Soldiers of the holy land, don't fret nor shed a tear.
We march toward that glory home that we should hold so dear,
And if we are to falter, stand up we can't stay here.
The marching of our footsteps fills all foes with fear.

Listen close, listen far, find where your enemies are:
Lurking in the caves, away from moons and stars.
You are the sons and daughters of a God of many wars.
Let your story and your song be sung above, raise the bar.

Soldiers of the holy land, don't you slow your stride.
The enemy is trembling, they've heard from far and wide:
You are a child of God that takes no devil's pride.
We're on the straight and narrow, and the Lord is on our side.

li.

What is the great mystery of invisibility?
To be invisible is to be unseen, yet ever present.

What is the great mystery of invincibility?
To be invincible is to be unstoppable and indestructible.

What is the great mystery of invisibility and invincibility?
It is that God has managed to be both.

lii.

Did you know the devil sweats?
I know, could've fooled me.
Always in the presence of heat,
You'd think it would not be.

But it should be known the devil's sweat is absolutely real.
The devil drips, soaking wet, when your weapon is revealed.

liii.

In a way, if you are chosen to be sick; it is because your faith is
    worrisome.
Not to you or to the common angel, but to the devil that
    challenges.
If you are a target in this battle, in this war, then you must be
    a threat.
That is one of many an explanation, for a sickened child of
    God.

Do not be worried if you are a target,
Embrace the challenge of the oppressor.
For a greater target from a greater artillery,
Aims primed at the heads of the dying enemy.

liv.

Do you know why the Lord fights from within you?
Because He always in-dures.

lv.

If you are sick, just know we are always sick.
For affliction comes in more forms than a virus.
Being sick, as we seem to be, means you're always healed,
for it is written as it was spoken, we must only believe.

lvi.

Humanity falls
As the fleeting circus does
But can be enjoyed.

lvii.

Sickness falls like rain
It pours, rejuvenating
And lasts just awhile.

lviii.

Fall, winter, and spring
Seasons of death and of life
All in perfect time.

lix.

Our days are numbered
Like syllables in a haiku
Fixed, indefinitely.

lx.

Is this not the end?
As long as the Lord tarries
Who can really say?

SCENE IV

· · · ·

LOVE AND HOW
TO FIND IT

lxi.

Meditate for just a moment on the things of God and life.
Carefully tread upon this ocean, it brings love and strife.

In the day of eternal thought, question not God's plan.
This only leads to the deepest darkness, where devils lurk with
     man.

As you walk upon the waters, only look to Christ.
The mighty waves come crashing still, but faith robs the heist.

The sea of man is growing fast, more turbulent and violent.
Know when God is in control, the presence of evil is silent.

It is not for us to understand the deepest depths of darkness.
For God takes care of all transgressions, in His sea: forgetfulness.

Stay above the turbulent waters, though they call to you.
Do not question nor run from God, or you will be taken too.

lxii.

Welcome to my fire, you must be a traveler too,
And if you'll sit for a moment you'll get, a story for multitudes.

Not a story that is scary, filled with devils, ghouls, or wraiths,
    but a story that is told for the Thief of Holy Faith.

One day, far away, a band of devils danced.
They gnashed their teeth and clapped their hands as the rascals
    haply pranced.
They cheered and twisted in the air, as their tails whipped by
    the fire,
A fire that was much like this, and they knew what would
    transpire.

"Oh, now we got 'em: these religious holy fools.
We picked 'em up and slammed 'em down, used them all as
    tools.
Now if they were smart, which we all know they're not,
They'd give up and accept their fate, 'fore their future gets
    mighty hot."

But as they flipped and flapped their wings inside the believer's
    soul,
A hooded man with contraband entered with one goal.
He stood and watched the devils, as the devils stopped their
    grins,
Standing oh-so-perfectly still, they knew he came to win.

"Now I know you know just who I am and what I understand,
And if you're smart, you'll surely start to run quick as you can.
This here soul you've decided to mole has always believed,
And upon that faith, I come to save, all who've been deceived."

The demons quickly pondered as they saw the hood of white,
pondered if today was the day they'd die in light,
and as the hooded man began to lift his hooded head,
The devils curled and hissed with fangs; they knew they'd soon
       be dead.

The man revealed His holy face, shining a mighty glow,
And in that moment was no atonement, for demons that do
       stow.
The demons curled and cowered, awaiting what He'd say,
For this was often characteristic, of the Thief of Holy Faith.

"Now why don't you just listen: go, get on your way,
For this here heart you've tried to smart is a home in which I
       stay.
If you try to come on back and steal my child away,
Just remember, I stole your power and quickly will again."

The demons took off running, clear and far away,
As that believer who prayed to Jesus won with Him that day.
As they ran, they remembered what brought Satan to his knees:
It was when Jesus walked into hell and took his deathly keys.

So now you know the story of this man who did the crime,
Of stealing back the keys of death, hidden for a time.
Thus, if you are haunted by devils, ghouls, or wraiths,
Don't you falter, go to the altar, meet the Thief of Holy Faith.

lxiii.

"Excuse me, sir, do you know where we are?"
"I don't think so, but what I know is that we're very far."

"It appears I'm lost. At what cost? Whatever will I do?"
"Do not fret, Coincident. I am here lost too."

"I will not judge or hold a grudge, for we are lost, No Better."
"That is so, let us go, and row this boat together."

lxiv.

Love is only forbidden because humanity's foolishness is not.

When does foolishness end and begin?

It ends and begins with God.

lxv.

To love another is to love one's self.
How can I see this, and you cannot?
You push away all love I offer,
insecure and broken.

I cannot fix you, nor wish to try,
I am only just a man.
I love myself, this is true,
but long to love you, pry.

But my love flew, overdue, no longer meant for two.
There is love, for many a dove, but certainly not for you.

I know you wish to love me as the feelings are shown: confession.
Friendly restriction and moral friction, cause your indecision.
Thus, I wait for our great day though my love will not.
When we say, in our own way, our love was all for naught.

lxvi.

Why do we love to tell such jokes? Jokes of ourselves.
Mocking, we act as kings, though we are only jesters.
We glorify being clowns, paint our faces with smiles and laughs
    as if we can't be seen for who we really are.

Illusions of fear draw ever near for the sadly happy master.
Instead of crying with one another, we chuckle, bloom, and
    bluster.
Instead of acknowledging our pain, we hide in a social cluster.
We give all before we fall, giving all we muster.

It's easy to laugh but not to cry,
I know this all too well.
It should be known the harder choice,
brings far better resolve.

Resolution is a dangerous thing, for it destroys our victimization.
Victims are comfortable, always cradled, like babies in the
    night.
They cry for the attention, the irony is searing, no mothers and
    fathers present.
Replaced they take the form of any with a voice.

Being a victim is damaging, for the fire burns nerve endings.
Eventually, you will not feel at all be entrapped like many.
Why accept a fate like this? Why limit yourself to pain?
Many choose to feel the fire, instead of feel the rain.

God takes in the many victims and turns them into warriors.
Perhaps you should give Him a try,
though you choose self-loathing.

Perhaps your pain will give a good laugh,
your media presence: reassuring.
But how long before the flame dies out?
How long before they leave you?

lxvii.

Dearest future wife,
Where art thou?
Hast thou chosen to torment me?
Do you hide in the tree or shadow?

I only wish to love you.

I know I may be ugherd and frankly quite dramatic.
But I am simply stricken by your beauty without and within.

Come to me mysterious spousal, I'll cherish thee for all time!
I know I'm not a chiseled statue, but alas, I am still cut.

Excuse my excitement, dearest love, I have loved you O' so
        long!
In a previous time before our own,
And now in times running short.

Dearest, come forth from the shadows,
I will marry us in an instant!
I only request your love in return,
For I, too, have been broken.

lxviii.

It's easier to defend a struggling man than a fool who chooses
   to struggle.
For some, struggling is part of their trials; for others, it is a
   lifestyle.

lxx.

Lord, help the people, for they are your people too.
Show mercy toward the foolish and peace to the distressed,
Comfort for the discomforted who are ever-needing.

Lord, help my family, for they're your family too.

Guide them toward the light, stand and fight for their fight,
Conquer their bitter battle, for good and for right.

lxxi.

Woman of great intrigue:
I only wish for conversation.
This conversation is only a piece,
of an overarching discussion.

Are we to be as one?
How can we be sure,
especially if we do not speak,
in truths as plain as day?

We are elaborate, not plain,
especially to our God,
for when He made you and He made I,
He made us extraordinary.

Here is our predicament:
We are stuck in ambiguity.
It's strange, I will admit,
but worth every fuss.

One day we'll speak of more than average,
make long of our short talks.
Send a glance in my direction,
though my brother abhors our love.

lxxii.

If I am to be a representative of God, how should I represent
    Him?
Many have been saints, and many have been sinners, but above
    all, most have been martyrs.

I do not know if I can withstand the forces of hell,
I do not know if I can die a martyr, for though many have lived
    to save countless souls,
many have failed and been executed.

lxxiii.

It is important to test the waters, especially ones of God,
For as many have been influenced by good, the same have been
    influenced by evil.

To be sure your influence is of God is ever so key.
Those who follow any leading will be locked out of heaven.

It is important to test the spirits, not all of them are holy.
Some are devils disguised as angels, for devils are angels fallen.

Test the waters of man, for a vast many have killed in God's
    name.
Be weary of those who speak freely, veering from the scripture.

lxxiv.

How outrageous to think we would judge another by their skin.
Like flowers, we are all plucked and placed in God's bouquet,
    collectively beautiful.

lxxv.

Alas, I am lovestruck, but who is it that has struck me?
I *feel* so strongly within, I swear it is love.

For every maiden that confronts me, not a one attains this
 feeling.
Though a few, out of the blue, send me surely reeling.

What is this love that I feel—this powerful affection.
It is a love for myself, a strange new love. I feel God's love
 within me.

If I am to love myself, and I myself am of God,
Then this most internal feeling is a love only He can give.

lxxvi.

If you're feeling lonely, if you're lost with undo,
cling to Jesus slowly, He will cling to you.

Though this road is rocky, and we will lose our way,
We must know that Jesus walks, on rocks or grass a-sway.

O Lord, I am yours, though I fight each day.
Through all my struggles, all my wars, I long to hear you say:

"O my child, you are mine, though lost you will be fine,
I have bought you in a time, today we face the grind."

Work me down when I am low, know all there is to know,
though rottings are reaped for what I've sown, your fruits show
      evermore.

lxxvii.

We are lucky devils are invisible.
I wonder if we could see,
If they would bear a close resemblance
To a friendly, familiar face.

lxxviii.

Do not condemn others with your command for repentance, especially if you do not know what must be repented.

lxxix.

I long to share a kiss with her; she's the one I love.
Not just a kiss on the marriage day, but a kiss to declare war.
A kiss of great affection, a kiss of unity.
To come together as one, facing all of hell.

In the great and mighty battle, we are warriors, both as one.
My partner and my jewel, to face hell's great opposers.
Let us fight in that great battle.
Let us march towards heaven.

SCENE V

·
·
·
·
·

LOVE AND THE
RETURN OF POLITICS

lxxx.

Love falls in hard times,
Like mana rains from heaven,
Slow but without end.

lxxxi.

Hello, strange friend,

     How long has it been, since I last spoke to thee?
I blame myself; it is my fault.
My convictions reign supreme.

I'm sorry for not loving you, as a best friend should.
Let us grow together, as one together would.

This great creation is yours, and our friendship is forever.
Despite the earth quickly fading, our love will have no end.

lxxxii.

"So who is she? Can I have a clue?"

"No."

"Why not?"

"You'll ruin the surprise."

"The surprise is ruining me."

"Grow up."

"I'd grow up faster with a hint."

"She is my daughter."

lxxxiii.

Dearest Barcelona,
    The times have been tough.
I must stress, I was a mess, and sure you're equally roughed.

There's little reason to explain, for a friend would understand,
but given the stakes, I will take a moment to expand.

I feel as though I've loved you for many years on end.
But I was dumb and ran to some though pretty, not a friend.

I've grown in maturity, with my love still intact.
So though I've played and long delayed, I hope this won't
impact.

For you and I, so strange and odd, explode with chemistry.
Though we wait, it's no debate, our fates are present history.

I hope to hear from you again; I know it's been a while.
Bring me bliss; it's you I miss. I'm sorry for the trial.

If you wish to try this out, please, write back.
Take my heart; its beat will start. Our hearts will stay intact.

lxxxiv.

But alas, Barcelona,
you never wrote back.

lxxxv.

"I'm having trouble expressing myself."

"What do you mean?"

"Emotionally. I feel like I refrain a lot."

"Do you know why that is?"

"I can't say I do."

"It's simple: You are afraid to love."

lxxxvi.

There is fear in the shadows, fear in the darkest mind,
one fear here to mention: fear of the Lord inside.

No sorrow, no pain, comes without gain.
Fear in the heart is lonesome; fear of the Lord still reigns.

Many times I have been beaten, broken, and abused.
The love of God gives me the token, and I love him with what's
    due.

No sorrow, no pain, comes without gain.
Though abandoned and disbanded, God's love falls like the
    rain.

So why is it we fear Him? Why is it we define?
His respect is owed Him. His blood's signed on the line.

There is no fear that I hold dear, outside this friend of mine.
If I love, I see the dove and let my love outshine.

No sorrow, no pain, comes without gain.
Loneliness fades, without dismay, I'll love you for all time.
As you yourself have loved me, I'll love, mirrored, with rhyme.

lxxxvii.

She has a most beautiful spirit.
For as much as she is beautiful on the outside, her soul shines
     ever brighter.

I am captivated by her in all her ways,
her personality, humor, love, and smile.

She is as genuine as the finest gold, great as the brightest beauty.
She is more than one I long for; she is my dearest friend.

lxxxviii.

I welcome you to the orb of the odd, a strange world not many
    understand.
You seem to know this orb quite well as though you are familiar.
Let us combine our strangeness together, for it is truly unique.

With great effort, I attempt rationality, and you pull my heart
    toward you.
You are a missing piece within this strange jigsaw puzzle;
You and I match perfectly.

We shall see what our world brings; you're a stranger like me.
Though we are similar, I feel I'm falling,
For someone I don't know.

How confusing: all these conflicting emotions and thoughts
    alike.
I only wish to find love, but how can I know for sure?
Perhaps you never can, and therein lies the risk.

Alas, I'll take a risk on you, despite what you might bring.
If you are to break my heart, God will mend it again.
Our love, if real, will glow: strange, bright, and true.
Or inevitably and graciously end, as fires surely do.

lxxxix.

If you are to break my heart, I will gladly have it broken.
You are worth every tear that I will surely shed.

xc.

In the midst of thought, I find myself in utter conflict.
Much like the world of which I live: fighting, destructive.
These thoughts commonly come in the ides of politics.
It's hard to escape such things, in a year of election.

As the date approaches, the walls are closing in.
What am I to do?
Be a patriot or be a believer?
Is it possible to be both?

Therein lies the conflict: am I to be a believer who loves his
    country or a patriot who loves what it stands for?
I suppose any believer would respect a country founded under
    God,
But for those who are not believers, it is all so different.

In a world so polarizing, and people so angry, politics and patri-
    otism turn to hate.
Discrimination reigns in every soul and burns as the hottest
    flame.

How am I to stand for my country?
As a believer, I feel as though I can't.
As a believer, I pray; as a believer, I love, but as a patriot?
I watch my country burn.

Socialism is a declaration of war, on freedom and on God.
If China can destroy believers and the Muslim man, what is to
say communism won't do that here?

If this war continues to rage, on spiritual and physical fronts,
then I should fight as a patriot and as a believer.
Though I wish to be unproblematic, the burning of Bibles has
made this my problem.
I'll do all I can, love fellow man, and those who do not want it.

I'm forced to stand at the ready, as war quickly approaches.
I defend my people and the not, the devil has made it so.

We must stand strong on what we believe; we must defend our
freedom.
The devils of communism come quickly, to destroy freedom
and God.

xci.

The pitfalls of corruption have spread to every sector of poli-
    tics, especially and foremost.
Therefore, the vote does not matter.
Our power is the Holy Ghost.

xcii.

But voting is a weapon nonetheless, though comparable to a
 pool noodle.
Yay, even pool noodles can keep us afloat in the deepest ocean.
This is to say: If we can do something, we might as well do it in
 the grand calculus of politics.
After all, it is better to float than it is to drown, regardless of
 how silly we seem.

xciii.

Yet a greater weapon in the hands of a believer is the word of
    God.
For a single vote can be rendered meaningless, though God's
    word cannot.
Vote if you must, but preach the gospel, for the gospel brings
    deliverance.
In the grander scheme of things, salvation beats the politician.

xciv.

But how are we to know God's word is God's word?
Many men have professed to speak for God, and the very same
    use God to bring their own corruption.
In a time of peril and thunder, how do we know what's God and
    what's not?
How do we know we are a tool of God, rather than the devil?

The answer, in some respect, is simple: We must follow the
    voice of God.
For the true prophet, ordained by the Lord, has come in His
    name.
Merry—in line with all of God's teachings—signs and wonders
    follow.
There is no doubt this is Elijah, he who is called Branham.

In times unsure, be sure of the word; stand upon it in your
    studies.
It is the rock amidst sinking sand; stay above the deathly pull.
The word, in its purest revelation, is individually found and
    individually believed.
Find Him in that secret place, read between the lines.

God loves each one in His kingdom and grows His community
    greatly.
All so different and all so beautiful, we are His, bed of roses.
Find Christ in His word; find the voice of God.
Use the sword He has given, held by the prophet.

XCV.

How many excuses can one believer make, before we stand up
    for God?
They march and mock Him in the streets, the one who died
    for us.
It would be unwise to charge the mob but would be wise to
    wise up.
Wise up to the challenge, wise up to the enemy, rise up to the
    occasion.

We must defend our Lord by being sure of what we believe.
If the mob can proclaim they are a movement who march
    against injustice,
Then we, as a body of believers, must march against the unjust.
Not in the realm of the physical, but of the spiritual no doubt.
If it's a war the devil wants, then it's a war the devil will get.

xcvi.

My God is gracious.
Thoughts worn like stone.
Love must stay within.

xcvii.

The mind stays crowded,
Though the heart rests in chaos.
Both keep me grounded.

xcviii.

She shines like a star,
Always present and beaming
Even in the dark.

xcix.

The poet is nothing more than a mortal.
Without anointing, we are nothing.
Gracious is the Lord for giving us what we need:
Purpose, inspiration, and divinity.

c.

There is love in the valley.
Love on mountains high.
Love that flows from the fountain,
Between you and I.

Oh, my Lord, my friend, ever present, begin and end.
You are like the lantern in the empty street:
Guiding us with your light.

There is no place I'd go if it were without you,
Greatest savior, God of salvation, God of love, inspiration.
The train named Investigation carries angels for our time.
God, you know I love you so and keep you deep inside.

There's love in the nation; love in this bride of mine.
The family of God: a kingdom, a nation formed inside.
Darkest caves, grimmest times, hinder not God's rhymes.
Look to father, mother, and daughter, each brings love in time.

There is sorrow, there is pain.
Teardrops fall like rain.
But God grows you as the farmland and showers you: the grain.

There is love in the people, believers and not alike.
Love in the gospel, let us reason with our lives.

If you wish to see me, my God shows what's in sight.
God the Savior, God the Healer, feed the hungry light.

If I am to die, I will not die a lie.
My God is truth, my God is life, who takes burden and strife.
He giveth deliverance and freedom,
And to the man a wife.

SCENE VI

THE BELIEVERS GET
THEIR FAIR SHARE

ci.

I have many times heard the people and their worldly
    condemnations.
Truly they have found an unhealthy obsession, and I have
    shared my grievance on this subject before.
But then, none would listen.

I will say this: If you are to condemn the world, then be ready
    to condemn yourself.
The Lord will not come until His bride has heard His voice.
Thus, upon this understanding, be careful the next time you
    warn others of the world's end.

Embrace in the speaking of God's word rather than shouting
    fearful threats.
For if their spirit dies, their blood is on your hands,
And you very well may join them.

cii.

Demons dance in the midnight moonlight.
Evil lurks in every corner.
Vile creatures make their mark,
In the purest righteous soil.

ciii.

Gracious are you in all your ways, overwhelming with your love.
Deliver all your children, make way your second coming.

civ.

Justice for all or none at all,
Ultimate fairness through Christ.
Liars wait among the crowd,
Invested in the art of murder.

Anxious and stressed, I lie in wait.
Never to falter, always to fight.
Let us come together,
Swiftly in the night.

CV.

"Tell me, boy, do you fear death?"

"I fear nothing of the sort."

"How can you be so sure? Do you know where you are going?"

"Do you?"

cvi.

If I had a stone for every high-horsed believer, I would not
     throw one myself.
I would reach to launch an angry rock and realize they'd all
     been taken.
Taken by every soul who cannot stand to be inferior.
They think themselves superior all because of God.

One should notice the irony in their statement before their
     horse is bludgeoned.
If you think of yourself as greater than man, then you think of
     yourself as God.
Those who think of themselves as God are in need of Him the
     most,
but no amount of condescension will bring Him to you.

I may not be one to throw the stones or even say a word,
but if you stay up on your horse, your brethren will knock you
     down.
If you call sinners "sinners," be sure you may cast a stone,
or be met by hundreds who'll hunt you and seek only your
     death.

cvii.

How sad, two parties can think themselves better because of
    their beliefs.
One side does not believe in God; the other condemns through
    Him.
But oh, you radicals of the religious and not, both of you are
    faulted.
Deep down, you are the same: You both are fueled by *hate*.

cviii.

To whom it may concern,

Understand I am not perfect. I am a man who speaks of his life,
in hopes it will bring Christ to others.
But be ye warned of what you say, concerning this book's
contents,
for though I am its author, I am not its author solely.

cix.

Is it foolish to fall in love?
Am I a foolish lover?
Why is it so difficult to love one another?

CX.

Why is it I attract those who will hurt me?
Is there a sign that's plastered on my face?
I think not, for I know my face quite well.
But do I know me?

Friends and family alike smell the blood of my lovingkindness.
The advantage is theirs in the water, I cannot help myself.
God made me this way, and some say I'm blessed,
But this blessing feels like a curse that calls to many hunters.

I am cursed to love those who love me not,
To give all I can to those who wish to take it.
Cursed to always fight for others though they desire to fight
    me.
Cursed, it seems, to live in pain.

This is my destiny.

How can this curse bring a blessing?
Is the blessing to love unconditionally?
What's in this blessing that I am missing
That is bestowed upon me?

cxi.

If Jesus loved those who crucified Him, shouldn't I love those
who abuse me?
As a believer, the answer seems simple, but as a man, the tor-
ment perplexes.

cxii.

There is but one issue on my mind today:
The fear of holy marriage.
I do not fear the idea itself, but the idea I'll be abused.
I'd much rather fear being alone than being with one of terror.

If it were to happen, I might love the most evil.
I know God has one for everyone,
I know He'll not leave us alone,
but are you aware that sometimes our person is meant to abuse
    us?

If you do not know, allow me to wash your muddied arrogance.
Some people are destined to love the abusive; they alone can
    handle it.
They're endeared as a human punching bag; they live and love
    like Christ.
It is an inescapable fate, for some of us, to love those who abuse.

cxiii.

You'll have to excuse my broken heart,
it's been broken before.
Though it's said a break grows strength,
the strongest can break again.

It'll happen one day or another,
by betrayal, change, or age.
One day, we'll lose those we love,
but with God, we'll see them again.

One day, that break will be the last,
for a heart can't take too much.
Breaks that happen time and time again,
take more time to heal.

But one day, the heart won't repair,
and, instead, will pass away,
and I, dear friends, as sad as it is,
grow wearier each day.

cxiv.

This is true: God loves the weary and repairs them over time.
However, I have a strange issue: My time is running out.

CXV.

Pain resides within.
Heartbreaks of past and present
Wash away with time.

cxvi.

Coal (under pressure) can become a diamond or break from the
severity.
What am I to be?
A diamond or broken?

cxvii.

Sometimes we're sad, and that's okay.
We can be happy another day.

cxviii.

The believer's heart is actively broken.
God specializes in such cases.
Why we choose this punishment,
I'll never know, but God is there nonetheless.

cxix.

Empty love from an empty heart cannot fill the heart's longing.
It is as a love note with no letter, which is to say it is empty.
Spare me your empty gestures; I seek what is real.
You have fed me nothing but lies and imitation.

CXX.

The greatest tragedy of all mankind is that you cannot save
    everyone.
Though we strive to do such things, it is not our duty.
The only One who can save is Christ,
we must be a part of Him.

As believers, we should be His representatives,
but we cannot save every soul.
Every soul is not ours to save; God is the savior.

Though we may march toward the enemy, we march past
    potential friendlies.
This thought, though painful, is important to rehearse before
    inevitable breaking.
It is a terrible thing to know that some people will be left in
    the past,
but we must carry on; we must be free at last.

SCENE VII

DEATH OF A POET

cxxi.

Notice:
I am no great poet.

In fact, to many, I will be seen as bad.
But I must remind you as I remind myself: I am just a man.
Do not focus on me; that is not the purpose.
Focus on what God is doing in the background and upfront.

cxxii.

Furthered:
Think of me as a character in a play, used to exemplify a moral.

For many lessons can be learned from the many well-written
   stories, and God is the best writer.

Though this book has poems of my life, telling tales from
   tumultuous times, look at them in the big picture, to
   understand the point.
Look not to the actor who is only acting; look to God to find
   the purpose.

We near the end of the story; the death of a poet.

cxxiii.

The first act calmly closes,
Lights and curtains come alive.
The stage is set for the closing chapter,
Ready your final bow.

cxxiv.

I walk onto the stage and face the audience, my shoes thud on
    the wood.
I've built it with my own actions and hands, over the course of
    time.

I am directed by God's direction, in perfect stage design.
I stand before the audience of heaven; the lights shine upon
    me.
In this moment of my final performance, I request one thing:
That I would go, not alone; that you would hold my hand.

CXXV.

cxxvi.

Muddied dark waters
Like sin in a believer's blood
be made clear and cleansed.

cxxvii.

How much darkness can I bare?
How long before I fail?
How will I survive with such demons against me?

Though Christ is the ultimate solution, my arrogance betrays
    Him.
Time is spent with any other.
Alone or with evils, I falter.

Though this darkness is a part of me, as darkness is with
    humanity, I am choosing to lose the fight,
to entertain demons rather than angels; thus, I must be stopped.

cxxviii.

Hollywood and all their idols are the fools that walk the earth.
They think they speak for those of us who, that poorly walk
    beneath them.
They claim they are oppressed, from inside their pearly
    mansions.
Still, we lend an ear to these fools as if they're gods.

We give them all their power, yet believe they empower us.
They are only jesters in the King's court; He rules over all.

God forbid any Hollywoodian make something great for God,
Instead, they bring awakening "wisdom" to the King and all
    His subjects.
Instead of being one of His own, they choose to mock Him as
    clowns,
Which, of course, as we all know, they absolutely are.

Since when did jokers become our rulers?
Since when were they qualified?
No genius is needed for modern film,
They all are quite dumb.

Why listen to these gold-plated diaper babies who grow their
    ivory tower?
All words they say to gain them virtue are empty, thoughtless,
    and irrelevant.

I would rather listen to someone who woefully walks beside
    me,
Than listen to someone who lords over, as a tyrant of utter
    villainy.

Christ walked beside the poor; He walked beside the thieves,
And still, though I act as a harlot, He walks beside the me.

His words are eternal and give such life,
Whereas movie star's are scripted.
They may shine in their starlight,
But they will never outshine the Son.

cxxix.

Oh, tweeters of the Internet, won't you come and save us?
You obviously know so much given all the things you say.

If you did not know what you said, you would not say such
    things.
You are so *brave* for all your paragraphs, spoken from the
    bluebird.

Call the millions to arms and burn all opposed,
Whether animate or inanimate, it makes no difference—they
    all deserve to go.

After all, you know best; isn't that right?
We should listen to you.

If you are the ultimate, I'd give you a chance as I give most
    people too.
Despite your lack of useful progression letting hateful ego
    ensue.

Now one thing stands of most importance that I'll bring to
    your attention:
Not that it *matters*, but you have abandoned God in your
    cause-o-cancelation.
A cause without Him is futile and inevitably will malfunction.

CXXX.

Cold
is
a
living member of Christ
who
will
stray
from
God.

cxxxi.

Cloud

                                                                    Cloud
                                                              Cloud Cloud
                                                    Cloud Cloud Cloud Cloud
                                                              Cloud

                        Cloud
                  Cloud Cloud Cloud
                        Cloud

                                          time
                                        greatest
                              the   for
                              is   a
                          mountain   higher
                              the   form
                            Atop   of
                      strengthening.   reflection,
                            is   for
                           and   if
                       impossible   you
                          not   can
                         is   conquer
                        it   the
                     climb   highest
                    to   mountain
                  hard   you
                   is   will
               Mountain   survive
                the   the
              Though   lowest

....t.......................................
..........................t..t..........

............V..A..L..L....E..Y......

...................t...
....t..............

cxxxii.

Walk with me through the valley.
Hold my hand in the presence of death.
Look in my eyes so we may share your comfort,
In this time of uncertainty.

As you walk with God, I do walk the same.
He is in you and He in I,
Let us grasp this revelation,
Let us fall in love, inside.

Though we are but only friends, I am asking for your presence.
A friendship is sometimes all that's needed in times such as
    these.
To fight the thoughts that plague us both, we must not walk
    alone,
For the loneliest journey we can ever take is walking solely
    home.

cxxxiii.

"Extra, extra, read all about it! Local poet makes poetic nonsensicals!"

"Poetic nonsensicals? What does that even mean?"

"I don't know. It's nonsense!"

cxxxiv.

Do I love the Lord?
I proclaim it as much before a human audience, nestled within
    the pews.

But do I truly love Him?
One could argue that I do, for everything I do is for Him,
But I could argue I love the people more than God Himself.

However, to love His people is to love Him.
My convictions blur my mind.
The devil knows all my bad acts,
Acted upon the stage set before heaven, being used against me.

More so, I use it against myself.
My own guilt and tragic thoughts sway me into places of uncer-
    tain and shaken faith,
Convincing me that I am unworthy.

Do I love the Lord if I am so easily shaken?
Perhaps, but this relationship is that of a parasite.
I am a leech who feeds off God's love, never to love Him back
    for more than a moment.

I am a thief who steals that which could be better given to
    someone deserving.
Surely that is a most definite lie but an interesting thought to
    be had.

God's love is for all, and all true love is of God.
Though I may diminish my birthright, I must remember that
  it is mine alone.

I suppose the trick is to learn to not abuse our inheritance,
To not abuse the Lord given every selfish act of act disbelief is
  a lashing upon His back.

My answer to the question of whether or not I love God is
  undoubtedly: yes.
The question is not whether or not I'm in love,
The question is, As a man, why do I struggle to show it?

CXXXV.

Dear God,

What is it that bothers me?
I know it cannot be too terrible though it feels that way.
A strange distance has grown between us.
One that refuses to leave and seems to be only further cemented
    by my loveless actions of self-loathing.

I feel You near me, and yet I still run.
What is it that pulls me away and instills this strange feeling of
    resentment?
It could be I find your methods harsh,
Though Your methods are only as harsh as the individual makes
    them.

Who am I to say? I am just a poet.
But You are God, the God, Creator of universes and Master of the
    unknown. I am but a speck of dust in the hourglass of time.
My problems seem insignificant, and yet I still complain and
    belittle myself to an end without meaning.
Should I blame my character? Should I blame You?

I know with certainty I desire your presence, the presence of
    the Creator; lover of souls.
Still, with this desire and You in my heart, I feel like I am miss-
    ing something.
I am missing something that I know not how to find, for I
    know not what it is.

cxxxvi.

A gift used is a gift discovered, but how does one venture into
    discovery?
Many dangers lie ahead, all continually misleading.
Many gifts can be used for good as well as evil,
We are not perfect, by any means, our internal conflict proves
    this.

However, our lack of perfection should not be used as a crutch
    but rather proof that we are children of God.
Though the mental tempest gives his best efforts to persua-
    sion, we should not give up.
Though we may be shaken, rattled, or discouraged, know it is
    all God's plan.
We are all a part of it even if we don't believe.

If we walk away, this truth turns into a lie, at least by our own
    understanding.
Calling God a liar is a dangerous thing, a thing I would not
    recommend.
I have spoken to those who walk in those shoes, and their feet
    bleed from their souls.
One cannot ignore the miles of busted glass that ribbons their
    hearts so.

The journey of self-discovery is long and never-ending and is
    more than this, often-times, hardly taken.
Reason being: the journey itself, though hard, is not as hard as
    coming to terms with our imperfections.

It is not as hard as realizing that in order to be better, we must discover our purpose.

We must realize, despite all we are going through or have done, we are beautiful in the eyes of God.

cxxxvii.

O Lord of the lonely, come listen to me.
I long to see you solely, be in your company.

cxxxviii.

Many trials lie ahead like the trial left behind.
All are designed to better our walk with Christ.

Highs and lows come ever near, as the changing and temperate
    winds.
Some flash wild and rip through the world, like the tornado or
    watery hurricanes.

Some winds are a gentle comfort, like the breeze in fall and
    spring,
Cooling the heat that has seen battle which rages from within.

We can predict what draws near, the same as we could for
    what's passed.
Which is to say, if anything at all, we predict very little.

It is not our place to know the future that is reserved for God.
All that we must know, yay believe, is that we are a part of it.

cxxxix.

I am a poet who longs to be heard by Christ.
Am I wrong for this?
This desire is fueled by ego yet balanced by self-awareness.

If I am not heard before my time, what will these works have
    been for?
I will not have failed myself but those who needed the gift.

However, many think me a fool and care not to hear the jester.
This is my fault alone and is a fault ever wide and empty.

Hear me humble reader, but not the me that is I.
Hear the gift I have within before I go to die.

cxl.

Forged by the fire, burned within the flame.
Death to the fighter, fighting in God's name.
Consumed not by darkness, nor by light of hellish flame.
I've been plucked from the fire, and I'll never be the same!

Kicked while we're down and punched while we're up,
Trying to do our best to fill our soulful cup.
Trampled over like the doormat in front of Satan's home, fight
     the oppressor, live forever, know you're not alone.

Journey through the fire, cry out Jesus's name!
Don't you tire, instead admire, God's timing's still the same.

You'll be plucked from the fire; He's never letting go.

The enemy won't give you compliments, but compliments
     aren't needed.
Half this world, barfed and hurled all good for lustful greedies.
Know God's blessed children, He hath interceded.
Give off your sweet savor, live your life now freely.

The enemy pushes sin, the temperatures run high,
God's hand reaches in as the devils start to fry.

We've been plucked from the fire, and we're never letting go!

Fin.

More by John Anderson

The Price of Salvation: Second Edition (coming February 2023)
The Price of Retribution (coming October 2023)
Lights (coming 2024)

ABOUT THE ILLUSTRATOR

Liz Gallego was raised in Phoenix, Arizona, and currently resides in Las Cruces, New Mexico. Liz is a self-taught oil painter and the proud owner of her small business, *Canvas No. 14*, in association with *Anderson Bookworks*. Her work is done with oil paint on canvas and takes on a voice of its own, being called abstract, spiritual, and undeniably beautiful. Though she may receive a lot of praise, her goal remains as simple as they are humble:

"I want to paint the world through my perspective. I want others to see the beauty I see."

ABOUT THE AUTHOR

John Anderson is a poet.

CPSIA information can be obtained
at www.ICGtesting.com
Printed in the USA
JSHW012052021222
34210JS00006B/41/J